The month of May, from the illuminated manuscript
Les Très Riches Heures du duc de Berry

The Story of a Special Day
Volume 141

May
20

140th day of the year
(141st in leap years)
225 days remaining
until the end of the year.

by Michael Dobson

Timespinner
Press

Table of Contents

Cover: Charles Lindbergh with the *Spirit of St. Louis* — for the *Event of the Day.*

Back Cover and Frontispiece: The month of May, from the French Gothic illuminated manuscript *Les Très Riches Heures du duc de Berry.*

May 20 Quotations

"I am, somehow, less interested in the weight and convolutions of Einstein's brain than in the near certainty that people of equal talent have lived and died in cotton fields and sweatshops."

— Stephen Jay Gould, died May 20, 2002

"It is so hard for us little human beings to accept this deal that we get. It's really crazy, isn't it? We get to live, then we have to die. What we put into every moment is all we have... What spirit human beings have! It is a pretty cheesy deal—all the pleasures of life, and then death."

— Gilda Radner, died May 20, 1989

"Only the insane take themselves quite seriously."

— Max Beerbohm, died May 20, 1956

"Never treat your audience as customers, always as partners."

— Jimmy Stewart, born May 20, 1908

"The usefulness of an opinion is itself matter of opinion."

— John Stuart Mill, born May 20, 1806

"Those who spend too fast never grow rich."

— Honoré de Balzac, born May 20, 1799

"I have come to believe that this is a mighty continent which was hitherto unknown."

— Christopher Columbus, died May 20, 1506

Event of the Day
Lindbergh Takes Off!

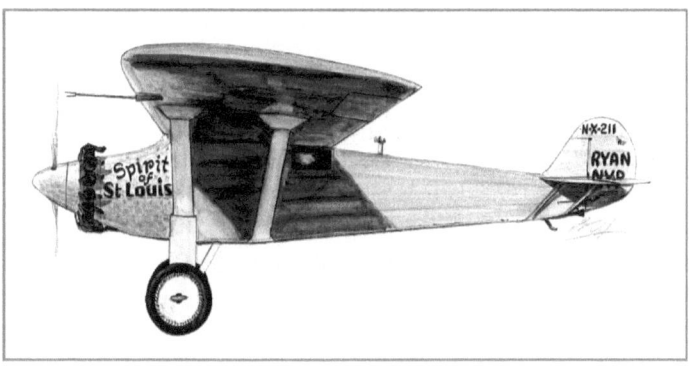

The Spirit of St. Louis

May 20, 1927, marks the takeoff of the Spirit of St. Louis, piloted by Charles Lindbergh, from Roosevelt Field, Long Island, for Paris. While the flight marks the first solo non-stop heavier-than-air flight from New York the Paris, it wasn't actually the first flight across the Atlantic.

The first aerial crossing of the Atlantic Ocean took place in May 1919. Three Curtiss NC flying boats made the 19-day journey in 50-mile jumps, with Navy destroyers strung out along the route from Nova Scotia to the Azores as beacons and docking stations. Only one, the NC-4, commanded by Albert Cushing Read, completed the journey. The plane is now at the National Museum of Naval Aviation in Pensacola, Florida.

Curtiss NC-4

The first nonstop transatlantic flight took place only a month later, when British aviators John Alcock and Arthur Whitten Brown flew a World War I-era Vickers Vimy bomber from Newfoundland to Ireland, winning a £10,000 *Daily Mail* prize. This was the first successful nonstop transatlantic flight, marred only slightly because the plane crashed on landing. That plane is on display at the London Science Museum.

One month later, the British airship R-34 (nicknamed "Tiny" by its crew), carrying a crew of 31 (plus two stowaways, one of them a kitten named "Whoopsie"), made the first round-trip crossing, from Britain to Long Island and back.

Later the same year, French-born New York hotelier Raymond Orteig attended a dinner honoring the World War I ace Eddie Rickenbacker, in which Rickenbacher expressed hope that one day the US and France would be connected by air. Inspired by the speech, Orteig decided to offer a prize — and like later New York magnate Donald Trump, named it after himself.

Putting up $25,000 in 1919 US dollars (the approximate equivalent of US$325,000 in 2011), the Orteig Prize would reward the first aviators to fly non-stop from New York to Paris, in either direction.

Although lighter-than-air transatlantic service run by the Zeppelin Company airline DELAG began in 1924, heavier-than-air technology lagged behind.

The first serious attempt at the Orteig Prize came in 1926, when Frenchman René Fonck and US Navy co-pilot Lt. Lawrence Curtin crashed their Sikorsky S-35 on takeoff. Two crewmen were killed.

Admiral Richard E. Byrd, famous polar explorer, announced his entry into the contest in late 1926. Heavily favored because of his previous achievements, Byrd purchased a modified Fokker C-2 monoplane, which he named America. It crashed on its first test flight.

Meanwhile, Clarence Chamberlin and Bert Acosta, flying a Bellanca WB-2 monoplane named Columbia, started practicing for an attempt at the prize, setting a world endurance record by circling New York City for over 50 hours. An official US Navy attempt at the prize ended badly when their aircraft crashed, killing both pilots, the week before they would attempt the crossing.

From the other side of the Atlantic, Charles Nungesser and François Coli in the Levasseur biplane *L'Oiseau Blanc* (White Bird) vanished in an attempt to win the prize.

But an unknown named Charles Augustus Lindbergh ended up the victor.

Charles Lindbergh and the *Spirit of St. Louis*

Lindbergh had been a barnstormer, a military pilot, and an airmail pilot, whose only distinction was holding the world's record for emergency parachute bailouts (four, a record that has been tied but never beaten). His safety record was so poor he had difficulty buying a plane, and was forced to have one custom-built.

Lindbergh was respected in the St. Louis aviation community, and so was able to obtain sponsorship from the St. Louis Chamber of Commerce. He raised $15,000 (just shy of $200,000 today) for the attempt

Ryan Airlines Corporation of San Diego, California, offered to build Lindbergh's plane for $6,000 ($76,000) — excluding the engine. He pledged to get the job done in three months. Lindbergh insisted on two, and on being the co-designer. Extra fuel tanks and an increased wingspan added range. Weight considerations meant the plane had no radio, no parachute, no gas gauges, and no navigation lights. Lindbergh even redesigned his boots to reduce weight, replaced the leather pilot's seat with a wicker chair, and reduced his maps only to those he'd use on the flight.

The entire venture almost ended before it started. Two days before Lindbergh was scheduled to leave San Diego for New York, Frenchmen Charles Nungesser and François Coli took off from Paris in the Levasseur biplane *L'Oiseau Blanc* (White Bird). All the other competitors stopped and waited to see if the Frenchmen would succeed — except for Lindbergh, who set off immediately for New York on his record-setting cross-country flight in the newly-named and christened Spirit of St. Louis.

When he reached New York, he learned that *L'Oiseau Blanc* had vanished. At the time, Nungesser and Coli's disappearance became as famous as the later disappearance of Amelia Earhart. (In recent years, evidence has suggested that the two men reached the North American continent before crashing, rather than having been lost at sea.)

That left two other competitors already in place at airfields on Long Island: Byrd and Chamberlin. Byrd's plane had a minor crash, delaying the attempt while repairs were made. Chamberlin's group was feuding over who would go on the trip. Lindbergh arrived on May 12, after having set a transcontinental speed record coming from San

Diego. He planned on a few extra days of testing —
the Spirit had undergone only 5-1/2 hours of test
flying because Lindbergh was in such a hurry.

Bad weather delayed all the crews, and it wasn't
until May 19 that the weather was good enough for
flying. However, the grass fields used for runways
were too muddy for a safe takeoff. Nevertheless,
Charles Lindbergh packed four sandwiches, two
canteens of water, and 451 gallons of gasoline, and
took off for Paris, barely clearing the telephone wires
at the end of the runway.

The 33-1/2 hour flight was fraught with danger.
Lindbergh flew through storm clouds and fog,
hampering his ability to navigate without
instruments. At 10:22 PM on Saturday, May 21,
Lindbergh landed at Aéroport Le Bourget, Paris,
where he was mobbed by 150,000 people who
dragged him out of the cockpit and carried him
around above their heads while souvenir hunters
tore off pieces of fabric for nearly half an hour until
French soldiers and police rescued him. Although
Lindbergh planned to fly back, President Calvin
Coolidge ordered the USS Memphis to ferry pilot
and plane back to America.

Following his return, Lindbergh made a goodwill
tour through the US and Latin America. In Mexico,
he met Anne Morrow, daughter of the US
Ambassador, whom he later married. The following
year, he donated the *Spirit of St. Louis* to the
Smithsonian Institution, where it hangs today in the
atrium of the National Air and Space Museum.

May 20 Holidays and Celebrations

Day of Remembrance (Cambodia)

The Cambodian Day of Remembrance (originally the "Day of Hatred Against the Genocidal Pol Pot-Ieng Sary-Khieu Samphan Clique and the Sihanouk-Son Sann Reactionary Groups") commemorates the beginning of mass killings in Cambodia by the Khmer Rouge regime that ruled the country between 1975 and 1979. It is marked by speeches, Buddhist ceremonies, and theatrical presentations.

The commemorative stupa at Choeung Ek (the "Killing Fields" is filled with 5,000 skulls.

Emancipation Day (Florida)

The state of Florida commemorates the
Emancipation Proclamation freeing slaves in the
Confederate states. Civil War reënactors act out the
May 20, 1865, speech announcing the Emancipation
Proclamation made by Union Major General Edward
McCook on the steps of the Knott House in
Tallahassee.

General Edward McCook, photo by Mathew Brady

European Maritime Day (European Council)

Established by the European Council, the European Parliament, and the European Commission in 2008, European Maritime Day seeks to raise awareness of the importance of the seas. An annual stakeholders confererence on May 20 marks the event.

Independence Day (Cuba)

Cuban Independence Day celebrates the island's independence from the United States on May 20, 1902.

Independence Day (East Timor)

The island nation of East Timor celebrates its formal independence from Portuguese rule in 2002. (It was actually occupied by Indonesia from 1975 to 1979, but it was still officially ruled by Portugal.)

Indonesian National Awakening (Indonesia)

In Indonesia, May 20 is *Hari Kebangkitan Nasional* or Indonesian National Awakening Day, a public holiday celebrating *pancasila*, the five principles of the Indonesian state philosophy: belief in the one and only God, a just and civilized humanity, the unity of Indonesia, democracy, and social justice.

Meck Dec Day (North Carolina)

Once an official holiday in North Carolina, Meck Dec Day commemorated the (historically disputed) signing of the Mecklenburg Declaration of Independence on May 20, 1775.

National Day (Cameroon)

Although Cameroon has no single date of independence, it celebrates its National Day on May 20 to commemorate the change from a federal system to a unitary country in 1972.

World Metrology Day (Metre Convention)

World Metrology Day celebrates the adoption of the metric system by 17 nations on May 20, 1875.

Christian Feast Days

In **Western Christianity**, May 20 is the feast day of Abercius and Helena, Aurea of Ostia, Austregisilus, Baudilus, Bernardino of Siena, Ivo of Chartres, Lucifer of Cagliari, and Sanctan.

In **Eastern Orthodox Christianity**, May 20 is the feast of Saint Lydia of Thyatira, martyr Thalelaeus the Unmercenary, Saints Zabulon and Susanna, Saint Mark the Hermit, Saint Dodo, Saint Thalassius the Myrrh-gusher, and the translation of the holy relics of Saint Nicholas the Wonderworker. (These events are observed on June 2 by "Old Calendarists.")

What Happened on May 20?

325 CE – **First Council of Nicea**

The first ecumenical council of Christian bishops formally opened May 20, 325 CE, in Nicaea, Bithynia (İznik in modern Turkey). It established many of the standard beliefs associated with Christianity, including defining the relationshp of the Son to God the Father, establishing the method for calculating the date of Easter, and writing the Nicene Creed.

1498 CE – **Vasco da Gama Discovers the Sea Route to India**

On May 20, 1498 CE, Portuguese explorer Vasco da Gama and a fleet of four ships arrived in Calicut, India, the first European navigator to achieve what Christopher Columbus and other had sought: a sea route to India.

1775 CE – **Mecklenburg Declaration of Independence**

May 20, 1775, appears on the North Carolina state flag, commemorating the signing of the Mecklenburg Declaration of Independence, claimed to be the first declaration of independence made in the American colonies. Its authenticity is disputed by historians.

Vasco da Gama meets the King of Calicut, India

1873 CE – **Blue Jeans Patented**

A German immigrant named Levi Strauss (rght), who had moved to San Francisco in 1853 to operate a dry goods business, partnered with tailor Jacob Davis to make work pants from denim cloth, using copper rivets at stress points to give the pants durability. They received US Patent 139,121 on May 20, 1873, for this invention, the beginning of blue jeans.

1875 CE – **The Metre Convention**

On May 20, 1875, a group of 17 nations signed a treaty to establish an international system of measurements, known as the metric system or the International System of Units (SI).

1899 CE – **First US Traffic Ticket Issued**

On May 20, 1899, the first traffic ticket in the United States was issued to New York City taxi driver Jacob German for speeding. He was traveling at 12 miles per hour.

1932 CE – **Amelia Earhart Takes Off**

Amelia Earhart became the first woman to fly across the Atlantic as a passenger in 1928, but wanted to set the record on her own. Taking off on the morning of May 20, 1932, from Newfoundland, she landed 15 hours later in Northern Ireland, becoming the first woman to make a transcontinental solo flight.

Amelia Earhart shortly after landing in Derry, Ireland

1940 CE – **First Prisoners Reach Auschwitz**

On May 20, 1940, a group of 30 German career criminals became the first prisoners of the newly-built Auschwitz concentration camp. During the camp's operation, between 1.3 and 3.0 million people, around 90% of them Jewish, would die there.

1941 CE – **Battle of Crete**

On the morning of May 20, 1941, Nazi Germany launched the first mainly airborne invasion in military history, attacking the Greek island of Crete. Although the Nazis were victorious after ten days of heavy fighting, the high casualty rate forced a reappraisal of their airborne fighting doctrines.

1956 CE – **First Hydrogen Bomb Airdrop**

On May 20, 1956, the United States made its first airdrop of a thermonuclear bomb, a 3.8 megaton strike against Bikini Atoll in the Pacific Ocean. The bikini bathing suit takes its name from this test.

1969 CE – **Battle of Hamburger Hill Ends**

The Vietnam War Battle of Hamburger Hill was a ten-day battle pitting the US and South Vietnam against the North Vietnamese military. A direct front assault against fortified North Vietnamese positions succeeded, but the hill was abandoned shortly after it was captured. This battle led to widespread criticism of the conduct of the war in the US Congress and forced a reappraisal of US strategy.

Who Was Born on May 20?

Business

Bill Hewlett (May 20, 1913 — January 12, 2001)

Bill Hewlett co-founded the Hewlett-Packard Company, commonly known as H-P.

William Fargo (May 20, 1818 — August 3, 1881)

William Fargo (right) was a key organizer of the companies Wells Fargo and American Express. The city of Fargo, North Dakota, is named for him.

Film and Television

Michaela McManus (May 20, 1983 —)

McManus played Lindsey Strauss on *One Tree Hill* and Kim Greylek on *Law & Order: Special Victims Unit*.

Candace Bailey (May 20, 1982 —)

Bailey co-hosted the TV program *Attack of the Show!* and appeared in the TV series *Jericho*.

Matt Czuchry (May 20, 1977 —)

Czuchry played Logan on *Gilmore Girls* and Cary Agos on *The Good Wife*.

Tahmoh Penikett (May 20, 1975 —)

Penikett played Helo on the Syfy series *Battlestar Galactica* and Paul in *Dollhouse*.

Timothy Olyphant (May 20, 1968 —)

Olyphant played US Marshal Seth Bullock in *Deadwood* and US Marshal Raylan Givens in *Justified*, and has appeared in numerous films.

Mindy Cohn (May 20, 1966 —)

Actress Mindy Cohn is best known as Natalie from the sitcom *The Facts of Life*.

Ted Allen (May 20, 1965 —)

Food writer Ted Allen is best known for his role on the TV series *Queer Eye for the Straight Guy.*

Tony Goldwyn (May 20, 1960 —)

Goldwyn was the voice of *Tarzan* in the Disney animated film, and starred as the President of the United States in the ABC TV series *Scandal.*

Bronson Pinchot (May 20, 1959 —)

Bronson Pinchot appeared in such films as *Risky Business* and *Beverly Hills Cop,* but is best known as Balki from the sitcom *Perfect Strangers.*

Dean Butler (May 20, 1956 —)

Butler is best known for playing Almanzo Wilder in the NBC TV series *Little House on the Prairie.*

Dave Thomas (May 20, 1949 —)

Comedian Dave Thomas is best known for his long-running involvement with the Canadian television series *SCTV.*

Anthony Zerbe (May 20, 1936 —)

Actor Anthony Zerbe's many films include *The Omega Man, License to Kill, The Turning Point,* and *Star Trek: Insurrection.*

David Hedison (May 20, 1927 —)

Actor David Hedison appeared in numerous movies and television shows, and is perhaps best remembered as the captain in the series *Voyage to the Bottom of the Sea*, and as the first actor to play CIA agent Felix Leiter in more than one James Bond film.

Betty Driver (May 20, 1920— October 15, 2011)

Actress Betty Driver appeared in over 2,800 episodes of the British soap opera *Coronation Street*.

George Gobel (May 20, 1919 — February 24, 1991)

Comedian George Gobel starred in the NBC weekly series *The George Gobel Show* from 1954 to 1960, and later appeared on numerous other TV shows.

Jimmy Stewart (May 20, 1908— July 2, 1997)

James Maitland Stewart was one of the greatest film stars of all time, appearing in numerous classic films from *It's a Wonderful Life* to *Rear Window*. He received five Academy Award nominations (one win) along with a Lifetime Achievement Award. He flew 20 missions as a B-17 pilot in World War II and rose to the rank of Brigadier General in the US Air Force Reserve.

Government and Military

Ron Reagan (May 20, 1958 —)

Radio host and commentator Ron Reagan is the son of US President Ronald Reagan.

Cindy McCain (May 20, 1954 —)

Businesswoman and philanthropist Cindy McCain is best known as the wife of US Senator and 2008 Republican presidential nominee John McCain.

Gerhard Barkhorn (May 20, 1919 — January 8, 1983)

Luftwaffe pilot Gerd Barkhorn was the second most successful fighter ace in history, credited with 301 victories on the Eastern Front out of 1,104 combat missions.

Gerhard Barkhorn's Messerschmitt Bf109 G-6

Moshe Dayan (משה דיין) (May 20, 1915 — October 16, 1981)

Moshe Dayan (right) was Chief of Staff of the Israeli Defense Forces and subsequently Minister of Defense during the Six-Day War (1967) and the Yom Kippur War (1973). He later served as Foreign Minister, where he helped draw up the Camp David Accords.

John Marshall Harlan II (May 20, 1899 — December 29, 1971)

Associate Supreme Court Justice John Marshall Harlan II served from 1955 to 1971, following his grandfather of the same name, who served on the Supreme Court from 1877 to 1911.

Faisal I (فيصل بن حسين بن علي الهاشمي) (May 20, 1885 — September 8, 1933)

Faisal I, along with Captain T. E. Lawrence (Lawrence of Arabia), organized and led the Arab revolt against the Ottoman Empire. He served as King of Syria for four months until overthrown by the French.

Subsequently, he served as the first King of Iraq until his death, where he was responsible for extensive modernization of his country. He also supported the establishment of a Jewish homeland in Palestine. He died at the age of 48 under suspicious circumstances.

King Faisal I of Iraq

Dolley Madison (May 20, 1768 — July 12, 1849)

Wife of fourth US President James Madison, Dolley Madison served as First Lady of the United States from 1809 to 1817. She also served as First Lady for ceremonial functions in the administration of second US President Thomas Jefferson, a widower.

Portrait of Dolley Madison by Gilbert Stuart

William Thornton (May 20, 1759 — March 28, 1828)

Inventor, painter, and architect William Thornton designed the United States Capitol and served as the first Architect of the Capitol. He was also the first superintendent of the United States Patent Office.

Literature and Philosophy

Mary Pope Osborne (May 20, 1949 —)

Children's book author Mary Pope Osborne is best known for her *Magic Tree House* series that has sold over 100 million copies.

Gardner Fox (May 20, 1911 — December 24, 1986)

Prolific comic book writer Gardner Fox created such characters as The Flash, Hawkman, the Justice League of America, and wrote for many comics titles, including Batman. He is credited with over 4,000 stories, many under pseudonyms.

John Stuart Mill (May 20, 1806 — May 8, 1873)

British political philosopher John Stuart Mill was highly influential in social and political theory, especially the theory of liberty.

Honoré de Balzac (May 20, 1799 — August 18, 1850)

French novelist and playwright Honoré de Balzac is considered one of the founders of the European realist movement, and influenced many other writers. He is best known for his multi-volume *La Comédie humaine (The Human Comedy)*.

Honoré de Balzac

Music

Busta Rhymes (May 20, 1972 —)

Rapper Trevor Smith adopted his stage name after NFL wide receiver George "Buster" Rhymes. He has received 11 Grammy nominations and has been called "one of hip-hop's greatest visual artists."

Susan Cowsill (May 20, 1959 —)

Susan Cowsill was the youngest member of the pop group The Cowsills.

Jane Wiedlin (May 20, 1958 —)

Wiedlin was rhythm guitarist for the rock group *The Go-Go's*.

Cher (May 20, 1946 —)

Cherilyn Sarkisian became famous as half of the pop duo Sonny & Cher (left), and went on to a highly successful solo career as a singer and actress, selling over 140 million records. She won the Best Actress Academy Award in 1988 for her role in *Moonstruck.*

Joe Cocker (May 20, 1944 —)

Singer Joe Cocker is best known for his Grammy-winning 1983 duet with Jennifer Warnes, "Up Where We Belong."

Shorty Long (May 20, 1940 — June 29, 1969)

Shorty Long co-wrote "Devil With the Blue Dress On" and "Here Comes the Judge."

Science and Invention

R. J. Mitchell (May 20, 1895 — June 11, 1937)

British aeronautical engineer R. J. Mitchell is best known as the designer of the Supermarine Spitfire fighter of World War II.

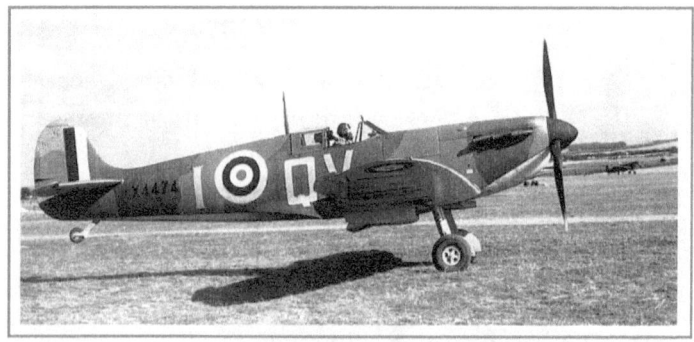

Supermarine Spitfire Mk I

Emile Berliner (May 20, 1851 — August 3, 1929)

German-American inventor Emile Berliner developed the disc record, or phonograph, and founded the well-known record label Deutsche Grammophon along with other companies. He was also a pioneer in the development of the helicopter.

Emile Berliner and the first phonograph

William Congreve (May 20, 1772 — May 16, 1828)

Second Baronet Sir William Congreve developed the famous "Congreve rocket," with a range of two miles but extremely poor accuracy. Congreve rockets are described in the US national anthem "The Star-Spangled Banner," in the phrase "And the rockets' red glare / the bombs bursting in air."

Sports and Competition

Kassim Osgood (May 20, 1980 —)

NFL wide receiver Osgood played for the Detroit Lions.

Jayson Werth (May 20, 1979 —)

Outfielder Werth played for the Washington Nationals, Toronto Blue Jays, Los Angeles Dodgers, and Philadelphia Phillies.

Ramón Hernández (May 20, 1976 —)

Hernández is an MLB catcher who has played for the Los Angeles Dodgers, Oakland Athletics, San Diego Padres, Baltimore Orioles, Cincinnati Reds, and Colorado Rockies.

Tony Stewart (May 20, 1971 —)

Racing driver Tony Stewart has been NASCAR Sprint Cup Series Champion, won the Winston Cup and the Nextel Cup, and is the only driver to have won a championship in both IndyCar and NASCAR.

Terrell Brandon (May 20, 1970 —)

NBA point guard Terrell Brandon played for the Cleveland Cavaliers, the Milwaukee Bucks, and the Minnesota Timberwolves in his ten year professional career.

Road Dogg (May 20, 1969 —)

WWE wrestler Brian James has won numerous championships and currently serves as a commentator on the web series *Are You Serious?*

Stu Grimson (May 20, 1965 —)

Enforcer Stu Grimson was known as "The Grim Reaper." He compiled over 2,000 penalty minutes in his 13-year career.

David "Boomer" Wells (May 20, 1963 —)

Former MLB pitcher David Lee Wells pitched the fifteenth perfect game in baseball history and subsequently became a sportscaster.

Bobby Murcer (May 20, 1946 — July 12, 2008)

After 17 seasons primarily with the New York Yankees, outfielder Bobby Murcer served as a sportscaster for the team for nearly 20 years.

Stan Mikita (May 20, 1940 —)

Chicago Black Hawks center Stan Mikita was elected to the Hockey Hall of Fame in 1983.

Ken Boyer (May 20, 1931 — September 7, 1982)

In his 15-year career as a third baseman for four different teams including the St. Louis Cardinals, Boyer won the 1964 National League MVP Award.

Bud Grant (May 20, 1927 —)

Head coach of the Minnesota Vikings, Bud Grant was named to the Pro Football Hall of Fame in 1994. He was the first coach in professional football history to have teams reach both the Grey Cup finals and the Super Bowl.

Bob Sweikert (May 20, 1926 — June 17, 1956)

In 1955, racer Bob Sweikert became the only driver to sweep the Indianapolis 500, the National Championship, and the Midwest Sprint Car championship in a single season.

Hal Newhouser (May 20, 1921 — November 10,1998)

Baseball Hall of Fame pitcher Hal Newhouser played with the Detroit Tigers and the Cleveland Indians in his 17 season career. He was considered the dominant pitcher of the World War II era of baseball.

Max Euwe (May 20, 1901 — November 26, 1981)

Dutch chess grandmaster Max Euwe won the World Chess Championship a record-setting twelve times in a row. He was president of FIDE, the World Chess Federation and wrote numerous books on chess.

Who Died on May 20?

Arts and Literature

Max Beerbohm (August 24, 1872 — May 20, 1956)

English essayist and caricaturist Max Beerbohm (left) is best known for his 1911 novel *Zuleika Dobson.* He was drama critic for the *Saturday Review of Literature*, gave radio talks for the BBC, and was knighted in 1939. He was also well known for his many caricatures of famous figures of the day.

Exploration

Christopher Columbus (before October 31, 1451 — May 20, 1506)

Although Christopher Columbus was not the first to discover the lands now known as the Americas (that honor goes to the Native Americans), nor even the first European (the Vikings beat him there), he was the first European to return with the news, and thus initiated the colonization of the New World.

Little is known of Columbus's early life, but he was an experienced trader when he first decided that it would be easier to reach India by sailing west across the Atlantic rather than east. He obtained financial support for a voyage from Queen Isabella and King Ferdinand of Spain for his famous three-ship expedition in 1492.

Although Columbus made four voyages across the Atlantic, he continued to believe until late in his life that it was part of Asia. It was later explorer Amerigo Vespucci who first concluded publicly that this was a new continent, which is why we know it as "America" today.

Detail from "Landing of Columbus" by John Vanderlyn

Film and Television

Jon Pertwee (July 7, 1919 — May 20, 1996)

Jon Pertwee played the third incarnation of the Doctor in *Doctor Who*.

Gilda Radner (June 28, 1946 — May 20, 1989)

Gilda Radner (right) was an original cast member of *Saturday Night Live*. Her famous characters include Roseanne Roseannadanna, Baba Wawa, and Emily Litella. She married actor Gene Wilder in 1984.

Music

Robin Gibb (December 22, 1949 — May 20, 2012)

Robin Gibb is best known as a member of the Bee Gees.

Jean-Pierre Rampal (January 7, 1922 — May 20, 2000)

Flautist Jean-Pierre Rampal is credited with making the flute more popular as a solo instrument than it had been since the 18th century.

Rudy Lewis (August 23, 1936 — May 20, 1964)

Rudy Lewis was inducted into the Rock and Roll Hall of Fame as lead vocalist of The Drifters.

Politics

Hamilton Jordan (September 21, 1944 — May 20, 2008)

Hamilton Jordan was Chief of Staff to US President Jimmy Carter.

Science and Invention

Eugene Polley (November 29, 1915 — May 20, 2012)

Engineer Eugene Polley is best known as the inventor of the wireless television remote control.

Stephen Jay Gould (September 20, 1941 — May 20, 2002)

Paleontologist and evolutionary biologist Stephen Jay Gould developed the theory of punctuated equilibrium. He became well known as a writer of popular science as a columnist for *Natural History* magazine, and his columns were collected into numerous best-selling books.

Sports

Randy Savage (November 15, 1952 — May 20, 2011)

Wrestler "Macho Man" Randy Savage held 20 championships in his long professional wrestling career.

"Macho Man" Randy Savage (Photo: Rob DiCaterino)

Syd Howe (September 28, 1911 — May 20, 1976)

Professional ice hockey left wing Syd Howe is in the Hockey Hall of Fame.

May
The Fifth Month

"Then came fair May, the fairest maid on ground,
Deck'd all with dainties of the season's pride,
And throwing flowers out of her lap around. ."

> — *Edward Spenser*, The Faerie Queene, *Book VII*

According to many scholars, the month of May takes its name from the Roman goddess Maia, an earth goddess who was the mother of Mercury. The poet Ovid, on the other hand, claimed that May took its name from the Latin *maiores*, meaning ancestors. In either case, the month of May in ancient Rome was marked by sacrifices to Maia, and her son Mercury was honored on the Ides of May (May 15).

May is the fifth month of the year in both Julian and Gregorian calendars. It was originally the third month in ancient Rome, because the new year began on March 1. Although Julius Caesar changed the length of several months during his great calendar reform (the Julian calendar), the length of May has remained constant at 31 days.

In the northern hemisphere, May occurs in the springtime, and in the southern hemisphere, May takes place in fall. Strangely, no other month begins or ends on the same day of the week as the beginning or ending of May, although January of the following year always begins and ends on the same day of the week as this year's May.

May in Other Cultures

In Latin and Old English, the month of May was named *Maius*, and it is *Mai* in French. In Arabic, the month is مايو, pronounced *māyū*. In Chinese, the equivalent month is 五月. Croatians call the month *svibanj* and in Czech it is *květen*. In Finland, it is *toukokuu*. The Jewish month of Sivan (סִיוָן) normally falls in May-June. It is the third month of the Jewish ecclesiastical year. The Irish called the month *bealtaine*, and it marked the beginning of summer. Slovenians call May *veliki traven*, or the month of the big grass.

May Superstitions

- May is an unlucky month for getting married.

- Never buy a broom in May.

- "Wash a blanket in May / Wash a dear one away."

- Cats born in May will bring snakes into the house.

- "Those who bathe in May / Will soon be laid in clay."

May Symbols

Birthstone: Emerald

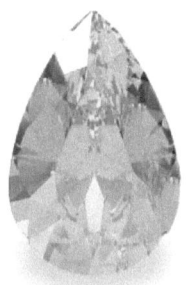

Birth Flowers: Lily of the Valley and Hawthorn.

Lily of the Valley   Common Hawthorn

May Events

Honorary Months

Presidents, Congresses, and nations around the world issue proclamations recognizing particular months to honor certain causes. These events generally fall in April. (All US unless otherwise noted.)

- American Bike Month
- Asian Pacific American Heritage Month
- Asparagus Month
- Drinking Water Month
- Jewish American Heritage Month
- Mental Heath Awareness Month
- Music Month (New Zealand)
- National ALS Awareness Month
- National Brain Tumor Awareness Month
- National Military Appreciation Month
- National Moving Month
- National Smile Month (United Kingdom)
- Older Americans Month
- Skin Cancer Awareness Month
- South Asian Heritage Month

Moveable and Multi-Day Events

Some events take place over a specific week or time period. Start and finish dates may vary from year to year. Some events occur on different days each year (such as "fourth Saturday of a month").

Victoria Day (Canada)

Victoria Day, a Canadian public holiday in honor of the birthday of Queen Victoria, is celebrated on the last Monday before May 25, meaning that it can occur as early as May 18 and as late as May 24, her actual birthday. It marks the unofficial beginning of summer in Canada.

Preakness Stakes (United States)

The second leg of horse racing's Triple Crown is the Preakness Stakes, held on the third Saturday in May each year at the Pimlico Race Course in Baltimore, Maryland. It can occur as early as May 19 and as late as May 23.

Vesākha (वैशाख)

The Buddhist holiday day known as Vesākha or simply Vesak commemorates the birth, enlightenment, and death of Gautama Buddha. It is celebrated on the first full moon of the month of Vesākha, which normally falls in April or May, and in leap years in the month of June.

May Zodiac Signs

From the perspective of someone on Earth, the Sun appears to move through the sky throughout the year, along a path astronomers call the ecliptic plane. The ecliptic plane is divided into twelve constellations, known as the zodiac, based on traditionally observed patterns of stars. On your birthday, you can't see your constellation, because it's part of the daytime sky.

The zodiac was first developed by Babylonian astronomers about 2,500 years ago. Because they were unaware that the Earth wobbles like a spinning top (a motion known as *precession*), they didn't make allowance for the fact that the Sun's path through the zodiac changes over time.

That means there are now two sets of dates for your birth sign. The *tropical* dates are the original Babylonian dates; the *siderial* dates tell you where the Sun actually appears as it moves along its annual path.

In both tropical and siderial reckoning, May 20 is in Taurus.

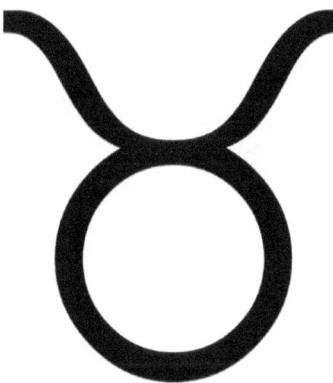

Taurus

Tropical April 21 to May 22

Siderial May 16 to June 15

In Greek mythology, Taurus was a disguise adopted by Zeus, who appeared to the maiden Europa in the form of a gentle white bull. Europa unwisely got too close, and Zeus kidnapped her to the island of Crete, where she bore him three sons, including Minos, builder of the labyrinth that housed the minotaur.

In astrology, Taurus is an earth sign, and Taureans are supposed to be quiet, gentle, compassionate, and stubborn. Taureans can appreciate the finer things in life and are cautious with money.

Illustration by Edward Penfield

What Day of the Week is May 20?

On what day of the week does May 20 fall?

Surprisingly, this isn't an easy question. Because the calendar year is 365 days long (366 in leap years), it doesn't divide evenly by the seven days of the week.

Also, the Earth goes around the Sun in about 365-1/4 days, so a calendar tends to drift over time. That's why the same date falls on different weekdays in different years.

This is made even more complicated by a change in calendars that took place in 1582. Our modern calendar has its roots in ancient Rome, in a calendar reform conducted by Julius Caesar. Caesar commissioned mathematicians to attack the problem, and they came up with the idea of *leap years*, and thus standardized the calendar for centuries to come. This was called the *Julian calendar.*

Over time, however, the small errors in Caesar's calculation compounded. That's why Pope Gregory XIII commissioned the *Gregorian calendar*, used in most of the world today. Some countries converted in 1582, when the calendar was first developed; some converted later; other still haven't changed.

Gregorian and Julian aren't the only types of calendars. The Hebrew year, the Islamic year, and many other calendars are used in different parts of the world and among different people.

You can convert Gregorian dates to other calendars, including the Hebrew calendar, the Islamic calendar, and even the Mayan calendar by visiting the Fourmilab Calendar Converter at http://www.fourmilab.ch/documents/calendar/.

Chinese calendar systems are quite complex and have changed several times; a full discussion is far beyond the scope of this book. If you're interested, you can find information here: http://www.hermetic.ch/cal_stud/chinese_cal.htm.

A 50-year brass perpetual calendar.

Copyright, Credit, and Contact

Follow Us

Our blog *Dobson's Improbable History* (http://
improbhistory.blogspot.com) features short articles
on events and people associated with each day, and
updates several times each week. You can also get a
daily "What Happened In History" message and all
the latest Timespinner Press news by following us on
Facebook at https://www.facebook.com/
TimespinnerPress. Our Twitter feed
@SidewiseThinker links you to all our News of the
Day.

Contact Us

Find an error or a format problem? Want information
about the series, about us, or about when the volume
for your special day might be available? Please email
us at editor@timespinnerpress.com. (We also take
requests.)

Editorial Notes

I worked at the Smithsonian Institution's National Air and Space Museum in the early 1970s as part of the team that built and opened the new facility on the National Mall in Washington, DC. The *Spirit of St. Louis* had been moved from its old home out to our restoration facility before going to its new home, and in the process some fabric from the airplane was removed and replaced. Each member of the staff received a certificate for having been part of the team that featured a square inch of the fabric from the *Spirit*. Mine is hanging in my home office.

On Dates

Historians use "CE" (Common Era) and "BCE" (Before the Common Era) instead of the more common "AD" (*Anno Domini*, or Year of Our Lord) and "BC" (Before Christ), reflecting the fact that the year-numbering system established by the Gregorian calendar is used throughout the world in many countries not culturally Christian.

The CE/BCE designation dates back to at least 1708, and have been adopted as a standard by the United Nations and the Universal Postal Union. Because this series of books covers events and people of all nations and cultures, we use the CE/BCE terms.

The abbreviation "O.S." on some dates refers to the fact that the Russian Empire did not switch from the Julian to the Gregorian calendar at the same time as the rest of Europe, and therefore some figures and events have two dates. (See "What Day of the Week…" for an explanation of Julian and Gregorian dates.)

People and events whose original names are not in the Western alphabet have their native names (where possible) in the appropriate script shown in parenthesis. If you are using an e-reader to access an electronic version of this book, all characters don't always display on all devices.

Sources and Art Credits

We owe a great debt to Wikipedia, which is our first stop for research. We attempt to make independent confirmation of all important dates and facts through a variety of other sources. Other sources we frequently use include the Library of Congress; "on this day" listings from *Encyclopedia Britannica,* the New York *Times,* and the BBC; and, of course, the always-useful Google.

All art and photographs are either in the public domain, used under a Creative Commons license, or with a "fair use" justification, and most frequently come from Wikimedia Commons and the Library of Congress Prints and Photographs Division.

Attribution is provided where requested by the copyright owner or when of historical significance, listed below. For information about any particular illustration or photograph, please contact us.

- The cover photograph of Charles Lindbergh with the *Spirit of St. Louis* is from the Library of Congress Prints and Photographs Division, and is in the public domain because it was first published in the United States between 1923 and 1963 and its copyright, if any, was not renewed.

- The illustration of the month of May used on the back cover and as the frontispiece is from the French Gothic illuminated manuscript *Les Très Riches Heures du duc de Berry* by the Limbourg Brothers, Jean Colombe, and an intermediate painter whose name is lost to history. It is in the public domain because its copyright has expired.

- The image of the *Spirit of St. Louis* was created by Steph Doyle, USAF Ret., and is in the public domain as a work of a U.S. Air Force airman as part of his official duties.

- The photograph of the Curtiss NC-4 is in the public domain as a work of the US federal government.

- The photograph of Charles Lindbergh and the *Spirit of St. Louis* is in the public domain as a work of the US federal government.

- The photograph of the monument at Choeung Ek was released into the public domain by its author, Quadell.

- The photograph of General Edward McCook was taken by Mathew Brady between 1860 and 1865, and is in the public domain because its copyright has expired. The image is from the Library of Congress Prints and Photographs Division, Brady-Handy Photograph Collection.

- The 1850 engraving of Vasco da Gama meeting the King of Calicut is in the public domain because its copyright has expired.

- The engraving of Levi Strauss is in the public domain because its copyright has expired.

- The photograph of Amelia Earhart at Derry, Ireland, is

in the collection of the National Library of Ireland. No known copyright restrictions exist.

- The 1862 portrait of William Fargo is in the public domain because its copyright has expired. The identity of the artist is unknown.

- The illustration of Gerhard Barkhorn's Bf 109 is by "Janmad" and used here under the CC BY-SA 3.0 license. An exemption to Section 86a of the German criminal code is claimed because the purpose is to report on a historically significant event, per Section 86, subsection (3). The same justification is claimed under the criminal laws of other countries that ban the use and display of Nazi symbols.

- The photograph of Moshe Dayan is cropped from an official White House photograph with Jimmy Carter. It is in the public domain as a work of the US federal government.

- The portrait photograph of King Faisal I of Iraq is in the public domain because its copyright has expired.

- The 1804 portrait of First Lady Dolley Madison by Gilbert Stuart is in the White House. It is in the public domain because its copyright has expired.

- The 1842 daguerrotype of Honoré de Balzac is by Louis-Auguste Bisson and is in the collection of the Institute de France. It is in the public domain because its copyright has expired.

- The 1971 publicity photograph of Sonny and Cher is in the public domain because it was published in the United States between 1923 and 1977 without a copyright notice.

- The 1940 photograph of a Spitfire Mk. 1 is in the public domain as a work created by the United Kingdom Government.

- The photograph of Emile Berliner with the first phonograph is in the collection of the Library of Congress Prints and Photographs Division. It is in the public domain because its copyright has expired.

- The 1897 caricature of Max Beerbohm by Max Beerbohm is in the public domain because its copyright has expired.

- The 1847 painting of Christopher Columbus landing in the West Indies is by John Vanderlyn, and is in the public domain because its copyright has expired. The original is in the collection of the Architect of the US Capitol.

- The 1976 publicity photograph of Gilda Radner (with Racquel Welch, cropped) from *Saturday Night Live* is in the public domain because it was published in the United States between 1923 and 1977 without a copyright notice.

- The 1986 photograph of Randy "Macho Man" Savage is by Rob DiCaterino, and is used here under the CC BY-SA 2.0 license.

- The photograph of an emerald was taken by Les Facettes and is used here under the CC BY-SA 3.0 license.

- The photograph of a lily of the valley (*convallaria majalis*) is by H. Zell and is used here under the CC BY-SA 3.0 license.

- The photograph of a hawthorn (*Crataegus monogyna*) is by Sannse and is used here under the CC BY-SA 3.0 license.

- The photograph of Czechoslovakian Easter eggs was taken by Jan Kameníček, who has released the image into the public domain.

- The photograph of the 1906 automobile calendar by Edward Penfield is from the Library of Congress Prints and Photographs Division, and is in the public domain because it was published prior to January 1, 1923.

- The 50-year perpetual calendar photograph is in the public domain.

License Description and Terms

Aside from material purely in the public domain, photographs and other material in this book are used under specific licenses permitting free use, usually with attribution. For full text and terms of these licenses, click or enter the appropriate links below.

- Creative Commons Attribution 2.0 Generic (CC BY 2.0): http://creativecommons.org/licenses/by/2.0/deed.en

- Creative Commons Attribution-Share Alike 3.0 Generic (CC BY-SA 3.0): http://creativecommons.org/licenses/by-sa/3.0/

- Creative Commons Attribution-Share Alike 2.5 Generic (CC BY-SA 2.5): http://creativecommons.org/licenses/by-sa/2.5/deed.en

- Creative Commons Attribution-Share Alike 2.0 Generic (CC BY-SA 2.0): http://creativecommons.org/licenses/by/2.0/deed.en http://creativecommons.org/publicdomain/zero/1.0/deed.en

- Creative Commons Attribution-Share Alike 1.0 Generic (CC BY-SA 1.0): http://creativecommons.org/licenses/by-sa/1.0/deed.en

- CC0 1.0 Universal (CC0 1.0) Public Domain Dedication (CC0 1.0)

- GNU Free Documentation License (GFDL): http://en.wikipedia.org/wiki/Wikipedia:Text_of_the_GNU_Free_Documentation_License

Timespinner
Press